Terrific
Toddlers

Bye-Bye!

by Carol Zeavin, MSEd, MEd
and Rhona Silverbush, JD

illustrated by Jon Davis

Magination Press • Washington, DC • American Psychological Association

American Psychological Association
750 First Street NE
Washington, DC 20002

With gratitude to my inspiring teachers and mentors at Bank Street, Rockefeller, and Barnard—*CZ*
Dedicated to the inspiration for this series, with infinite love—*RS*
For Laura and Greta—*JD*

Magination Press is a registered trademark of the American Psychological Association.
Order books here: www.apa.org/pubs/magination or 1-800-374-2721

Book design by Gwen Grafft
Printed by Worzalla, Stevens Point, WI

Library of Congress Cataloging-in-Publication Data
Names: Zeavin, Carol, author. | Silverbush, Rhona, 1967– author. | Davis,
    Jon, 1969– illustrator.
Title: Bye-bye! / by Carol Zeavin, MSEd, MEd, and Rhona Silverbush, JD ;
    illustrated by Jon Davis.
Description: Washington, DC : Magination Press, [2018] | Series: Terrific toddlers
Identifiers: LCCN 2017038182| ISBN 9781433828768 (hardcover) |
    ISBN 1433828766 (hardcover)
Subjects: LCSH: Separation anxiety in children—Juvenile literature. |
    Separation anxiety—Juvenile literature.
Classification: LCC BF724.3.S38 Z43 2018 | DDC 155.44—dc23 LC record
    available at https://lccn.loc.gov/2017038182

Manufactured in the United States of America
10 9 8 7 6 5 4 3 2 1

Sometimes mommies and daddies say bye-bye.
"See you later!"
"I'll be back soon!"

Sometimes it's hard to say bye-bye.

Sometimes JoJo cries.
"I want my mommy!"
Her mommy says,
"I see you're sad.
I'll miss you too,
but I'll be back...

...right after you go to the park.

Mommy always comes back."

Sometimes Kai wails,
"No go, Daddy!"
His daddy says,
"I see you're worried.
But I'll be back...

...right after you play at school.

Daddy always comes back."

Sometimes Ava yells,
"No! No bye-bye!"
Her daddy says,
"I see you're mad.
But I'll be back...

...right after your lunch and a nap.

Daddy always comes back."

Sometimes Jack just
holds his mommy tight.
His mommy says,
"I see you don't want me to go.
But I'll be back...

...right after your dinner and bath.

Mommy always comes back."

When mommies and
daddies come back, they
give us a big hug and kiss.
They smile and say,
"I'm happy to see you!"

Mommies and daddies always come back.

Note to Parents and Caregivers

Bye-byes are hard. For everyone. Now imagine that you're still relatively new to the world and utterly dependent on—and in love with—your parents. You don't yet have a firm sense of the permanence of people and objects. You don't have a sense of time. You don't understand your feelings. And you don't have the language to express any of this. Welcome to your toddler's experience.

We know we're stating the obvious when we say that a parent's leave-taking is extremely upsetting to a toddler. You have—we know—the empirical evidence to prove it. Toddlers will express themselves according to their individual personalities: sob hysterically, have big tantrums, withdraw, throw things. Grief, rage, sadness, fear—all the powerful emotions we recognize in our older selves are also present in our small toddlers, often at the most inopportune times, like when we are trying to leave.

Unfortunately, what to do during leave-taking is not at all obvious. In fact, it's counterintuitive. We adults are conditioned to "soothe" by saying, "It's OK. Don't worry. It's not a big deal." But your departure is a big deal to your toddler, and saying it isn't actually adds insult to injury. Anxious feelings don't go away by avoiding them or distracting from them. While this approach may be more comfortable in the moment, it amounts to telling your toddler that these feelings aren't authentic—which only adds your toddler's feeling misunderstood to the good-bye experience!

And remember, toddlers don't yet understand the emotions they are experiencing and don't have the vocabulary to identify these emotions or to share them with others...which adds to their frustration...which further heightens their emotional state...which in turn results in—yep—heightened behavior as well.

So in nuts-and-bolts terms, what can adults do?

Acknowledge the feelings. Give the feelings a name. "I see you are sad" ("angry," "upset," etc.). When we give our toddlers a vocabulary for what they're feeling, they can see their experience as concrete and manageable. Communicate that it's OK to feel sad, frightened, or angry.

Keep calm. At the same time, while you the adult are taking the child's emotions seriously, you yourself should stay calm and try to be matter-of-fact about this highly charged experience. Remember, you are their model—your toddlers take their emotional cues from you.

Give a time frame. Since young children don't have a sense of time (really, what's a minute or an hour to a toddler?), use "child time" ("after lunch," "after your bath") to give your toddler a concrete idea of when you'll return.

Create a consistent "I'll return" refrain. Toddlers don't know that you will return. Routines help your toddler know what to expect, and are reassuring. Use a constant refrain for leave-takings, such as, "I love you, and I'll be back," or "Mommy/Daddy always comes back." These regularly repeated phrases will serve as a verbal security blanket for your toddler to hold onto. Create your own, and say it every time.

Keep it short. Keep it real. You can do this.

Carol Zeavin holds master's degrees in education and special education from Bank Street College, worked with infants and toddlers for nearly a decade as head teacher at Rockefeller University's Child and Family Center and Barnard's Toddler Development Center, and worked at Y.A.I. and Theracare. She lives in New York, NY.

Rhona Silverbush studied psychology and theater at Brandeis University and law at Boston College Law School. She represented refugees and has written and co-written several books, including a guide to acting Shakespeare. She currently coaches actors, writes, tutors, and consults for families of children and teens with learning differences and special needs. She lives in New York, NY.

Jon Davis is an award-winning illustrator of more than 70 books. He lives in England.